Seattle World School
Seattle, Washington

REVOLUTIONARY DISCOVERIES OF SCIENTIFIC PIONEERS™

THE LAWS OF GENETICS AND GREGOR MENDEL

FRED BORTZ

ROSEN
PUBLISHING®

New York

Published in 2014 by The Rosen Publishing Group, Inc.
29 East 21st Street, New York, NY 10010

Library of Congress Cataloging-in-Publication Data

Bortz, Fred, 1944– author.
The laws of genetics and Gregor Mendel/Fred Bortz.—First edition.
    pages cm.—(Revolutionary discoveries of scientific pioneers)
Includes bibliographical references and index.
ISBN 978-1-4777-1806-3 (library binding)
1. Genetics—History—Juvenile literature. 2. Genetists engineering—History—Juvenile literature. 3. Geneticists—Biography—Juvenile literature. 4. Mendel, Gregor, 1822–1884—Juvenile literature. I. Title.
QH437.5.B67 2014
571.8'5—dc23

2013016384

Manufactured in the United States of America

CPSIA Compliance Information: Batch #W14YA: For further information, contact Rosen Publishing, New York, New York, at 1-800-237-9932.

A portion of the material in this book has been derived from *Mendel and the Laws of Genetics* by Heather Hasan.

CONTENTS

INTRODUCTION

"She has her mother's eyes." "He's the spitting image of his dad." "The twins have their grandfather's crazy sense of humor."

How many times have you heard people say things like that? When you think about it, it would be surprising if people—or any living things—did not resemble their parents and relatives. That's called heredity, the passing of traits from one generation to the next.

We humans have known about heredity for a long time. And we have used it ever since civilization began. For thousands of years, we have controlled the way domesticated animals mate to create different breeds of sheep, goats, cows, horses, dogs, cats, and other animals. These breeds have traits that make them more useful or appealing to us. We have also learned how to select seeds from plants with more desirable traits and grow them for food or other purposes in agriculture and industry.

Most of what we learned was by trial and error. Only in relatively recent history have we understood the science behind heredity. That science began in the mid-nineteenth century with the work of an Austrian monk named Gregor Mendel (1822–1884). In his monastery garden, he discovered that there were units of inheritance that produced different traits in pea plants. Later, those units came to be called genes, and the science of genes came to be known as genetics.

IN THE GARDEN OF HIS MONASTERY, AUSTRIAN MONK GREGOR MENDEL EXPERIMENTED ON PEA PLANTS TO SEE HOW CERTAIN TRAITS WERE PASSED FROM ONE GENERATION TO THE NEXT. HE DISCOVERED THAT THERE WERE UNITS OF INHERITANCE ASSOCIATED WITH DIFFERENT TRAITS. WE NOW CALL THOSE UNITS GENES, AND WE CALL THE SCIENCE THAT MENDEL BEGAN WITH THOSE EXPERIMENTS GENETICS.

Mendel's work launched a revolution that is still going on. Yet his work was little known in its time and was nearly lost for more than three decades. Today we know that genes are carried inside the cells of every living creature, from the simplest single-celled organisms to the most complex plant and animal species. We know that they are passed along as a chemical code written on molecules called deoxyribonucleic acid, or DNA. And we know how to take apart and reassemble DNA in ways that challenge our understanding of life itself.

This is the story of both Mendel's quiet life and the scientific revolution launched by his work in a monastery garden. It is a revolution that has produced both promise and controversy far beyond anything Mendel could have imagined.

BECOMING A SCIENTIST

Gregor Mendel was born to Anton and Rosina Mendel in Heinzendorf, a village in a region of central Europe then known as Moravia, in July 1822. He lived in a time when the principles of modern science were just being discovered. More than a decade earlier, English scientist John Dalton (1766–1844) had published *A New System of Chemical Philosophy*, a breakthrough text that described matter as comprised of atoms that come together to form molecules. Only a year before Mendel's birth, another Englishman, Michael Faraday (1791–1867), had begun his groundbreaking work on electricity and magnetism. These fields would grow to maturity at the same time Mendel did.

Historians believe the exact date of Mendel's birth was probably July 22, although the baptismal

IN JULY 1822, ANTON AND ROSINA MENDEL WELCOMED THEIR SECOND CHILD AND ONLY SON INTO THE WORLD IN THIS HOME IN THE SMALL VILLAGE OF HEINZENDORF, MORAVIA (NOW PART OF THE CZECH REPUBLIC AND CALLED HYNČICE U ODER). THEY NAMED HIM JOHANN. AS AN ADULT, HE BECAME A MONK AND TOOK THE NAME GREGOR. THE HOME IS NOW A TOURIST ATTRACTION.

register shows his birthday as July 20. His parents named him Johann. Only later, when he became a monk, would he take the name Gregor. Moravia was in the middle of the former Austro-Hungarian Empire, and Heinzendorf was a small village of only seventy-two households. Today, this town is known as Hynčice u Oder and is part of the Czech Republic.

Mendel grew up as the middle child—and only son—in a family of three children on a small plot of land on which his father grew fruit trees and raised bees. Although the family was relatively poor, they had enough money to replace their wooden house with a more expensive brick one. They also owned two horses. Part of Mendel's house still stands today, and visitors can see a memorial dedicated to him.

There was plenty for young Mendel to do on the farm to help his father. As a boy, he helped his father farm their land, but he was not destined to be a farmer like his father. It could have been on that farm that Mendel developed his love for science. Perhaps it was while he worked on the farm that Mendel first noticed patterns of heredity among the livestock. One thing was certain: Mendel loved learning.

AN EXCEPTIONAL STUDENT

Mendel was fortunate that there was a school in his town of Heinzendorf. Many of the other towns in the region had no schools at all. He began attending the village school as soon as he was old enough. It did not take long for his teachers to notice that he was an exceptionally intelligent boy.

Because he was a gifted student, Mendel's teachers recommended him to a school in Leipnik, Moravia (now known as Lipník nad Bečvou, Czech Republic), so he could prepare to attend the gymnasium, or high school. The gymnasium provided an education only for the best students, those few who would go on to study at a university. Children who did not attend the gymnasium learned a trade, such as farming or wood-working.

Mendel's parents wanted the best for him. Although they were poor, they managed to scrape up enough money to send him to the gymnasium in 1834, when Mendel was about twelve years old. Mendel's success, however, was hard on his parents, and it was hard on Mendel, too. The gymnasium was in Troppau (now Opava, Czech Republic) and was too far from home for daily travel. Mendel had to live there, and it was very expensive. His family could afford to pay for only half the normal amount of food. He must have suffered from more than a few pangs of hunger, although his parents sent him bread and other foods from their farm whenever they could.

Mendel's parents also had to deal with the fact that he would not be taking over the family farm when his father grew older. Then, in 1838, Mendel's father was seriously injured while working. This situation placed a lot of stress on young Mendel. His parents were no longer able to pay for any of his schooling, leaving him to support himself entirely. Perhaps due to stress or depression, Mendel became quite sick with a mysterious illness and stayed in bed for several months.

Mendel decided to study to become a teacher so that he could make money by tutoring while he continued his education. In the material that Mendel submitted as part of a job application, he wrote about how difficult it was to have to support himself at the young age of sixteen.

TOWARD UNIVERSITY STUDIES

Mendel attended a course at the teachers' seminary in Troppau. He was then able to make a small amount of money tutoring his classmates. After graduating from the gymnasium in 1840, Mendel decided to enter the Philosophical Institute at Olmütz (now Olomouc, Czech Republic) to complete two years of philosophical study. This education included the history of philosophy as well as mathematics.

Mendel, however, had little money and was unable to find tutoring jobs in Olmütz. Now desperate, he once again took to his bed with illness, this time staying there for a year. This pattern would be repeated throughout Mendel's life whenever he was faced with difficult circumstances.

Fortunately, Mendel's sisters came to his rescue. His older sister, Veronica, had married, and her husband agreed to purchase the family farm. This not only provided Mendel with money but also relieved him of his guilt over not taking care of the farm himself. Mendel's younger sister, Theresa, offered him her dowry, the money that had been set aside for her future marriage. Mendel was so grateful to his younger sister that he later supported the schooling of her three sons.

With the money that his sisters had provided, Mendel was able to complete his two-year study at the Philosophical Institute. There he studied religion, philosophy, ethics, pedagogy (teaching methods and techniques), mathematics, and physics. However, the money was not enough to allow him to fulfill his dream of attending a university. Mendel later wrote in his autobiography that he no longer wanted to have to struggle. Mendel's physics professor at the Philosophical Institute, Friedrich Franz (1783–1860), who was also a priest, urged him to become a monk. Mendel knew that this was the only way that he would be able to obtain an education because the monastery would send him to a university.

ENTERING THE MONASTERY

Mendel requested admission into the Augustinian monastery of St. Thomas in Brünn. In those days, Brünn (now known as Brno) was the capital of Moravia. Friedrich Franz recommended Mendel to the Augustinian abbot, the head of the monastery. Franz's recommendation called Mendel one of his best students. Mendel was accepted, and he joined the monastery on September 7, 1843, at the age of twenty-one. Because it was

IN 1843, MENDEL ENTERED THE AUGUSTINIAN MONASTERY OF ST. THOMAS IN BRÜNN (NOW KNOWN AS BRNO), SHOWN HERE IN THIS MODERN PHOTOGRAPH WITH THE BASILICA ASSUMPTION OF OUR LADY TO THE RIGHT. FOUR YEARS LATER HE BECAME A PRIEST. HE SOON DISCOVERED HE WAS NOT WELL SUITED TO TRADITIONAL CHURCH DUTIES, SUCH AS VISITING THE SICK. SO THE HEAD OF THE MONASTERY ARRANGED FOR HIM TO BECOME A TEACHER, WHICH ALSO ALLOWED HIM TIME TO STUDY SCIENCE.

traditional for monks to change their names when they entered the monastery, he took the name Gregor.

Mendel was ordained into the priesthood in August 1847. He was soon assigned various church duties, such as visiting sick patients in the hospital. It quickly became clear that Mendel was not fit for

WHY MENDEL CHOSE THE PRIESTHOOD

From a twenty-first-century perspective, entering a monastery seems to be an unusual choice for a scientist, but it was not that unusual in the Austro-Hungarian Empire in the mid-1800s. Sons who would not inherit their father's land had few options for making a living. Their only choices were often to join the army or a religious community. Since monasteries were often places of intellectual activity, Mendel saw it as a place where he would have an opportunity to gain an education.

This was true of the Augustinian order, especially after 1807, when Emperor Francis I decided that the Augustinian monks of St. Thomas were to take over the teaching of mathematics and religion at Brünn's Philosophical Institute. Mendel's mathematical abilities made him a perfect fit for the monastery.

MENDEL LIVED MOST OF HIS ADULT LIFE IN THE AUGUSTINIAN MONASTERY OF ST. THOMAS IN BRÜNN. BY THE 1860S, HE HAD RISEN TO THE POSITION OF ABBOT. IN THIS PICTURE, HE IS STANDING SECOND FROM THE RIGHT, HOLDING A FUCHSIA IN BLOOM, THE SYMBOL OF HIS POSITION THERE.

these duties. He became very upset and ill whenever he visited the patients. Mendel also still desperately wanted to teach because teaching would allow him time to study science.

It was obvious that Mendel was better suited to teaching. For this reason, Abbot Cyrill Napp (1792–1867), the head of the monastery, wrote a letter stating that Mendel would take a position teaching mathematics and literature at the secondary school at Znaim (now known as Znojmo). Mendel was thrilled with this change. He began teaching in 1849, even though he did not yet have a formal document from a university approving him to do so.

Mendel excelled as a teacher. He made his lessons exciting and easy to understand, and the children loved him. In 1850, a new law required teachers to pass an exam to be certified. Even though Mendel was very intelligent and did well in the classroom, the exam covered topics in the pedagogy of science that he had not learned. He had to leave teaching to study those topics at the University of Vienna.

SHAPING A SCIENTIST

Although Mendel was sent to the University of Vienna to learn how to teach science, he was more interested in the science itself. He studied physics, chemistry, zoology (the study of animals), and botany (the study of plants) with many of the best scientists of the time. He studied experimental physics with the world-famous Austrian physicist Christian Doppler (1803–1853). Doppler is most famous for describing the Doppler effect, which explains how the frequency of light and sound waves shifts when the source is moving. You probably hear his name in weather reports, when forecasters say wind patterns have been measured with "Doppler radar."

Another brilliant professor at the university was physicist and mathematician Andreas von Ettingshausen (1796–1878). His work remains important in modern physics, especially in regard to systems with many small parts that interact with each other, such as the molecules in a gas or fluid. It is also important for statistical analysis, an area of mathematics that Mendel later used to explain the results in his heredity experiments.

What Mendel learned from his botany professor, Franz Unger (1800–1870), was also significant for the future. Unger made a strong impression on Mendel. Unger was one of the most controversial biologists of the time. In his *Botanical Letters to a Friend* (1852), Unger said that he believed plants gradually changed over generations. This went against what the church believed at that time. The church's position was that nature remained exactly as God originally created it, as described in the Bible. Because his ideas differed from what the church believed, Unger was threatened with dismissal from the university.

Unger also introduced Mendel to the work of another scientist named Mathias Jacob Schleiden (1804–1881). Schleiden discovered that all plants and animals are made up of cells. This was also a revolutionary idea at that time. Unger greatly deepened Mendel's interest in botany and inspired him to study heredity in plants.

Mendel returned to Brünn in the summer of 1853. The following year, he was assigned as a teacher at the Brünn *realschule*, similar to a high school today. In 1856, he again tried to pass the teacher exam, but he was so anxious that he had an emotional breakdown and failed. Though that failure was a great disappointment at the time, it led Mendel to a new focus in life—doing science rather than teaching it—and pointed him toward a revolutionary discovery that we are still exploring today.

CHAPTER TWO

MENDEL THE LEADER

Although Mendel was a modest man, his intelligence and broad interests made him a leader in science, among his fellow priests, and in the community. In the 1850s, Brünn, with a population of seventy thousand, had a vibrant culture and was one of the fastest-growing cities in Europe. Its population came from many different backgrounds and spoke many different languages.

Mendel was very active in the social and cultural life of the town. He was first vice president and then president of the local mortgage bank. Mendel was also elected to committees on education, roads, and, perhaps most important, agriculture. Brünn's economy was built around the land. Farms produced cash crops, vineyards and orchards produced fruit, and pastures supported flocks of sheep.

ALTHOUGH THIS BRÜNN STREET SCENE IS FROM 1896, IT IS LITTLE CHANGED FROM WHAT MENDEL EXPERIENCED DURING HIS YEARS IN THE AUGUSTINIAN MONASTERY THERE. NOT ONLY WAS HE A LEADER IN HIS RELIGIOUS COMMUNITY, BUT HE ALSO PLAYED AN ACTIVE ROLE IN THE SOCIAL, ECONOMIC, AND CULTURAL LIFE OF THE TOWN.

That may account for Mendel's interest in heredity and why he chose to study plants in his own research. But Mendel's natural curiosity also led him to many other areas that were important in science, business, and everyday life, such as the weather. He was a founding member of the Austrian Meteorological Society.

MENDEL AND AUSTRIAN POLITICS

The political system of feudalism still existed in the early nineteenth century in the Austro-Hungarian Empire, where Mendel lived. It was a relic of the Middle Ages and did not officially end until 1848. In feudal society, people belonged to one of two classes, the nobles and the peasants. The king gave land to his most important nobles. These people were referred to as lords. The peasants lived and worked on the land of the noblemen, who offered them protection from potential invaders. In exchange, the peasants earned enough to buy the barest necessities.

Mendel was fortunate enough to grow up in a village that was part of the estate of Countess Maria Walpurga Truchsess-Zeil, a noble who cared about the peasant children on her land. It is because of her that Mendel was able to go to school as a young boy. And school was where Mendel's brilliance was first noticed. Had he grown up under a less enlightened noble, Mendel's life might have been quite different.

Looking back at that time today, it is easy to see the inequalities of the feudal system. But the peasants did not know any other kind of life. It took many years for discontent to reach the point of rebellion, but in 1848, a revolutionary movement finally spread throughout the Austro-Hungarian Empire. People wanted more civil liberties, such as the right to vote, the right to write what they wanted, and the right for workers to go on strike. They also wanted an end to feudal labor.

At the time, Mendel was living in the monastery. Mendel's life as a monk was barely affected by the revolution since the monastery was under church control. However, Mendel did sign—and, according to recent scholarship, may have written—a petition demanding full citizenship for monks. Under the feudal system, monks lost all their civil rights when they entered the monastery. The petition that Mendel signed was ignored, but the end of feudalism in the Austro-Hungarian Empire was announced on March 13, 1848.

BIOLOGY BECOMES A SCIENCE

At the beginning of the nineteenth century, people began to realize the importance of science. Even the Moravian Catholic Church shared this feeling. So the monastery of St. Thomas was a great place for a gifted man like Mendel to be. He was encouraged by the empire, the church, and the abbot to study whatever sciences he found interesting. For Mendel those included meteorology, physics, botany, and mathematics.

Mendel and the other monks were also fortunate to have all the materials that they needed at the monastery. The Augustinian monastery of St. Thomas, like other religious institutions at that time, received money from

MENDEL AND OTHER SCHOLARS FOUND LIFE IN THE AUGUSTINIAN MONASTERY ATTRACTIVE IN PART BECAUSE OF ITS WELL-STOCKED LIBRARY. IT INCLUDED BOOKS DESCRIBING THE LATEST RESEARCH IN THE SCIENCES, EVEN WORKS LIKE THOSE OF JEAN-BAPTISTE LAMARCK AND CHARLES DARWIN THAT CHALLENGED CHURCH DOCTRINE ABOUT HOW SPECIES CAME TO BE. TODAY, THAT LIBRARY CONTAINS OVER TWENTY-SEVEN THOUSAND VOLUMES.

the local farms. With this money, they bought scientific instruments, plants to study, and other useful tools.

Mendel's monastery also had a well-kept library, which contained books on many different subjects. Mendel made good use of the library. Every morning he got up at six o'clock and went straight there to study. Most important, however, Mendel had access to an experimental garden inside the monastery. The original colored drawings of the plans for the greenhouse still exist today and show its size and shape. It was there that Mendel carried out his experiments and sought to explain the mysteries of heredity.

Until the nineteenth century, scientists considered the study of plants (botany) and the study of animals (zoology) as separate fields. But as the century turned, so did the scientific vocabulary. The word "biology," meaning the science of life and combining botany and zoology, first appeared in print during that period. It was used in an 1802 book called *Hydrogéologie* by the notable French scientist Jean-Baptiste Lamarck (1744–1829).

LAMARCK AND DARWIN

Lamarck thought of the natural world as a staircase, with every living thing striving to become more complex, moving up the steps of the staircase. How did living things become more complex? Lamarck believed that they reacted to their environment, developing new traits that improved their capabilities as living organisms. He argued that parents could then pass those new traits, as well as the traits that they were born with, down to their offspring. Lamarck suggested that these acquired changes gradually turned a species, or a specific type of animal or plant, into a new species.

LAMARCK AND DARWIN BOTH THEORIZED THAT SPECIES CHANGED OVER TIME, BUT THEIR IDEAS WERE QUITE DIFFERENT. LAMARCK WROTE THAT LIVING ORGANISMS ACQUIRED NEW TRAITS, SUCH AS THE GIRAFFE'S LONG NECK, THAT ENABLED THEM TO THRIVE IN THEIR ENVIRONMENT *(UPPER PANEL)*. THEY THEN PASSED THOSE ACQUIRED TRAITS ALONG TO THEIR OFFSPRING. DARWIN'S THEORY *(LOWER PANEL)* RELIED ON NATURAL SELECTION, IN WHICH INDIVIDUAL ORGANISMS COULD ONLY PASS ON INBORN TRAITS. HE ARGUED THAT THOSE WHOSE TRAITS WERE BEST SUITED TO THEIR ENVIRONMENT WERE MORE LIKELY TO SURVIVE TO HAVE OFFSPRING.

These ideas angered many religious leaders of the time because they contradicted their interpretations of the Bible. They believed that the Bible was true in every detail and that God created the universe, including all species known today, in six days about five thousand years ago. But as much as Lamarck's ideas upset them, Charles Darwin's 1859 book *On the Origin of Species* angered them even more.

Darwin accepted Lamarck's idea that species changed but not in the way Lamarck suggested. He did not agree that organisms could pass acquired traits to their offspring. His extensive research showed that there was variation among organisms. He theorized that a process, which he called natural selection, determined which of those different traits would be passed on from one generation of organisms to the next.

Darwin noted that having a certain trait might make an organism more likely to survive and have offspring than another that did not have that trait. For example, an animal with speed might be better adapted to its surroundings by being able to outrun its predators. This animal would then have a better chance of surviving long enough to produce offspring with that same trait. Over time, the favorable trait would become more and more common among members of the species.

Even though the scientists of the nineteenth century, like Lamarck and Darwin, were interested in heredity, there were still questions that they were unable to answer. Darwin's theory of natural selection explained how particular variations in a species gradually became fixed traits of that species over the generations. However, he incorrectly assumed that the different traits of parents were blended together to create the offspring in the same way that paint colors blend when different paints are mixed.

It was a sensible interpretation, but it turned out not to be the way heredity works. Three years before Darwin's *On the Origin of Species* shook the world of biology, Mendel had begun work on a set of experiments that would cause another revolution in the life sciences. But unlike Darwin's work, which spread quickly around the world, Mendel's would go almost unnoticed for decades.

REFINING DARWIN'S BIG IDEA

Darwin's work revolutionized biology, and Mendel read Darwin's books carefully. His personal copies of *On the Origin of Species* (1859) and *Variation of Animals and Plants under Domestication* (1868) had pencil notes in the margins and on the back covers. Even though Mendel was a priest, he had no problem accepting evolution. Because he had grown up on a farm, he understood that farmers bred their animals and selected their seed plants to favor certain useful traits. The farmers weren't going against nature; they were using it.

But Mendel's knowledge of agriculture also led him to doubt one aspect of Darwin's theory. As a young boy on the farm, he had observed how vegetables, fruits, and animals passed down their traits from one generation to the next. Mendel agreed with Darwin that organisms inherited traits from their parents and that this could lead to evolution over many generations. But he disagreed with Darwin that parents' traits are blended in their offspring.

He had seen that some traits seemed to get passed on while others did not. Did the traits of the parents compete with each other, or did they combine with each other to produce a characteristic in an offspring? These were the questions that Mendel sought to answer, and he turned to the garden pea for answers.

WHY MENDEL CHOSE PEAS

When Mendel returned from the University of Vienna, he found himself overseeing some of the community food gardens for the monastery. One of the main crops grown in these gardens was peas. The garden pea, or *Pisum sativum* by its scientific name, was a great organism for Mendel to study for many reasons. For one, the pea plant is very easy to grow. The plant is self-fertilizing and is able to produce offspring without ever coming into contact with another plant. It is able to do this because each plant contains both male and female reproductive parts. However, it is also easy to crossbreed, or mate different varieties, of these plants in an experiment. Sets of offspring are produced relatively quickly, so it doesn't take long to get experimental results. The offspring then grow to maturity in a single season.

There were many varieties of peas available to Mendel. In fact, at the monastery today, visitors can still see lists of seeds that Mendel ordered. Each variety of pea plant differed from the others in several traits that were easy to identify, such as height, pod shape, and seed color.

Mendel decided that he could learn more about inheritance by deliberately crossing the different va-rieties of garden peas. By seeing what traits the off-spring of the crosses pos-sessed, he could figure out how traits are passed down from parent to offspring. In preparation for these exper-iments, he scribbled com-ments in his copy of Carl Friedrich von Gärtner's book *Versuche und Beobachtun-gen über die Bastarderzeu-gung im Pflanzenreich* ("Ex-periments and Observations on Hybridization in the Plant Kingdom"), which had been published in 1849.

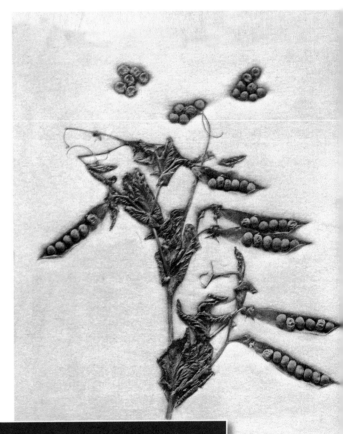

DARWIN THEORIZED THAT PARENTS' TRAITS WOULD BE BLENDED IN THEIR OFFSPRING, BUT MENDEL'S RESEARCH ON PEAS SHOWED A DIFFERENT RESULT. BY CROSSING A ROUND GREEN PEA WITH A WRINKLED YELLOW PEA, MENDEL FOUND THAT THE OFFSPRING WERE EITHER GREEN OR YELLOW, NOT A COLOR IN BETWEEN, AND EITHER AS SMOOTH OR AS WRINKLED AS THE PARENTS, NOT SOMEWHAT LESS WRINKLED.

A NATURAL LABORATORY

Mendel used the garden as a natural laboratory. He chose seven characteristics of the pea to study. These included the shape of the seeds (round or wrinkled); the color of the seeds (yellow or green); the shape of the pea pod (smooth or bumpy); the color of the pea pod (green or yellow); the color of the seed coats (gray or white); the position of the flowers on the plant (all over the stem or only at the tip); and the length of the

MENDEL CARRIED OUT HIS FAMOUS EXPERIMENTS ON THIS SMALL PLOT OF GROUND AND IN THE MONASTERY GLASSHOUSE. THE RESULTS WERE ALMOST LOST TO HISTORY, BUT WHEN THEY WERE REDISCOVERED IN THE EARLY TWENTIETH CENTURY, THEY SET OFF A REVOLUTION IN BIOLOGY AND LAUNCHED THE NEW SCIENCE OF GENETICS.

stem, or the height of the plant (tall or short). He later included flower color, too (purple and white).

With the support of Abbot Napp, Mendel began his experiments with the pea plants in 1854 in the monastery garden and glasshouse, or greenhouse. Mendel filled the long tables in the glasshouse with pots of pea plants. In each pot, he planted seeds that would grow to show one of the seven traits he had chosen to examine.

For the first two years of his experiments, Mendel worked to make sure he had pure-breeding plants. Plants that are pure-breeding for a trait will always produce offspring that have that same trait, generation after generation. For instance, a pure-breeding plant that has wrinkled seeds will produce a line of offspring that have only wrinkled seeds. Mendel wanted to make sure the plants were pure breeders because he planned later experiments with crossbreeding.

THE EXPERIMENTS BEGIN

Mendel chose to mate pea plants with opposite traits. That is called crossing. For example, in one set of experiments, Mendel carefully chose a group of pure-breeding tall plants. He then crossed, or mated, those tall plants with pure-breeding short plants. He did this by transferring pollen by hand from the tall plants to the short plants. With tweezers, he opened up the part of a plant that held the pollen and then used a tiny paintbrush to carry the pollen to the other plant.

Mendel took the seeds that these plants produced and planted them. He named these his first generation of plants (or F1 generation). As the seeds grew into plants, he was able to see what characteristics they had inherited. Would they be tall or short? You might expect that some of the plants would be tall and some would be short. Or maybe you would think that the offspring would all be medium-height plants since tall and short plants were crossed. But Mendel observed something altogether different. When the offspring of the tall and short plants grew, Mendel saw that they were all tall!

Crossbred plants are called hybrids, meaning the offspring of parents with different characteristics,

HOW CROSSBREEDING EXPERIMENTS WORK

Peas, like many flowering plants, have both male and female parts in the same flower. The male parts produce pollen, and the female parts, called ovaries, receive it. That process, called fertilization, produces fruits and seeds that can produce new plants.

When Mendel did his first crossbreeding experiments, he transferred pollen from pure-breeding plants for one trait (such as round seeds) to the ovaries of plants that were pure-breeding for the opposite trait (wrinkled seeds) to see what traits their offspring displayed.

such as one tall and one short. Although it seemed as though the short trait had disappeared in the hybrids, Mendel soon found that it had not. Mendel allowed the tall hybrids to self-pollinate. When he planted their seeds and allowed them to grow to produce the second generation of plants (or F2 generation), he found some of the offspring were short.

Because of his mathematical training, Mendel began looking at these results in terms of probability and ratios. For instance, in the F2 generation, he noted that tall plants and short plants occurred in a three-to-one (3:1) ratio. In other words, for about every three tall plants, there would be a short plant. Mendel saw the same pattern with the other characteristics he was observing. For instance, when he crossed a plant with round seeds with a plant with wrinkled seeds, all the first-generation plants had round seeds. However, if these round-seeded plants were allowed to self-pollinate, about one-fourth of the second-generation offspring had wrinkled seeds.

For eight long years, Mendel worked diligently, crossing thousands of pea plants. Imagine the time it must have taken Mendel to sort, count, and record information about every pea from each different trait. He kept careful notes on what he did and what he observed. Finally, as a scientist should, he presented his results to a scientific society in 1865 and published them in a scientific journal the next year so others could learn from his research and build on it.

MENDEL WORKED FOR YEARS, CROSSBREEDING DIFFERENT VARIETIES OF PEAS, EXAMINING AND RECORDING THE TRAITS OF THOUSANDS OF PLANTS, THEIR PODS, AND THE SEEDS THEY CONTAINED. BECAUSE HE THOUGHT MATHEMATICALLY, HE WAS ABLE TO RECOGNIZE AND INTERPRET THE MEANING OF STATISTICAL PATTERNS OF INHERITANCE.

In science, presentations and publications are only the first steps in a long process of discovery. The information has to reach those other scientists who can best learn from it. And those scientists have to see its value and follow up with their own research and publications.

Unfortunately, no one followed up on Mendel's findings, and he was soon assigned to another position that ended his research. His results were almost lost to history. They were rediscovered only in 1900 when other scientists who had performed similar experiments began to publish their results. They recognized that their research provided important insights into how traits pass from parents to offspring. So when they reviewed the older literature, they were astonished to discover that an unknown monk working alone had beaten them to press by thirty-five years!

CHAPTER FOUR

A REVOLUTION DELAYED

*M*endel's work had interesting parallels to Darwin's, but their lives took very different paths. Both scientists had notebooks full of data based on work they had done over many years. And both had come to revolutionary conclusions based on their data. Darwin proposed a theory that species evolved through heredity, guided by natural selection of certain inherited traits over others. Mendel developed a theory that explained how heredity worked. Together, those theories are the foundation of modern biology, but the two scientists became prominent in different ways.

FAME VS. OBSCURITY

Darwin began giving lectures to important groups and publishing interesting results from his notebooks almost as soon he returned from a famous round-the-world voyage on a ship called the *Beagle.* Yet it took nearly thirty years before he felt satisfied that his theory of evolution was complete enough to make public. By then he was well known, and everyone paid attention to his book *On the Origin of Species*, especially his most severe critics. The controversy that erupted over its conclusions only

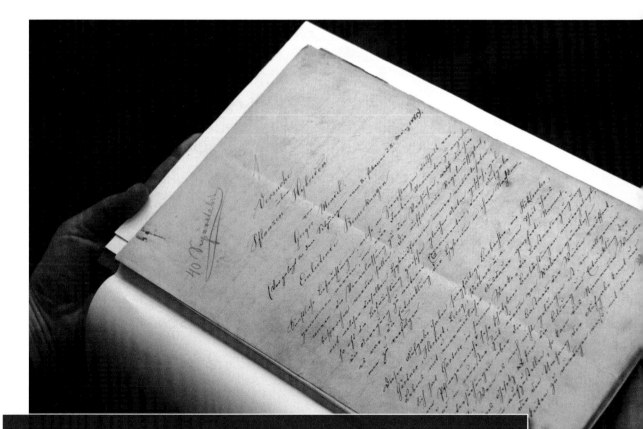

UNLIKE CHARLES DARWIN, WHOSE WORK WAS FAMOUS LONG BEFORE HE PUBLISHED *ON THE ORIGIN OF SPECIES*, MENDEL WORKED IN OBSCURITY. ALTHOUGH IT IS NOW REGARDED AS A HISTORIC SCIENTIFIC BREAKTHROUGH, MENDEL'S PAPER "VERSUCHE ÜBER PFLANZEN-HYBRIDEN" ("EXPERIMENTS ON PLANT HYBRIDS") RECEIVED LITTLE ATTENTION BECAUSE ITS 1866 PUBLICATION WAS IN THE MINOR JOURNAL *PROCEEDINGS OF THE NATURAL HISTORY SOCIETY OF BRÜNN.*

enhanced Darwin's scientific reputation and spread the theory worldwide.

Mendel did not think about publishing anything until he had completed his full set of experiments with peas in 1863. And when he finally did, hardly anyone noticed. Lacking Darwin's fame, and working in an obscure monastery rather than in London's high society, Mendel was at a great disadvantage.

Finally, in 1865, Mendel presented his results to the Natural Science Society in Brünn. That group did not carry much importance compared to the groups that heard Darwin. And unlike Darwin, Mendel was not a captivating presenter. His report was so lengthy that he had to go back a second time to finish presenting it. And the members understood little of what the long-winded monk was saying.

Mendel's obscurity was only part of the reason his work was barely noticed. In many ways, Mendel was ahead of his time. He had brought the laws of probability to the study of heredity. Mendel had used his mathematical skills to look for patterns in the results of his crosses. He had counted, for example, that 253 self-fertilized F1-generation plants produced 5,474 smooth seeds and 1,850 wrinkled seeds. In another instance, he counted 6,022 yellow seeds and 2,001 green seeds in an F2 (or second) generation.

The numbers would have meant nothing if Mendel had not understood what the statistics meant. Mendel had noted that in all his crosses, the ratio of one trait to the other in the second generation was very close to three to one. This ratio suggested that the makeup of an individual offspring was a matter of chance that could be expressed in mathematical odds.

Never before had anyone used mathematics to explain biology. Despite their lack of understanding, the society members invited Mendel to publish his results in their journal *Proceedings of the Natural History Society of Brünn*. Mendel's paper "Versuche über Pflanzen-Hybriden" ("Experiments on Plant Hybrids") appeared in the society's journal a year later, in 1866. Unfortunately for Mendel, the journal was not widely read because the society that published it was small and not well known.

Mendel also sent copies of his paper to many well-known biologists of the time. He waited anxiously for a reply from any one of these scientists, but his only response came from a German biologist named Karl Wilhelm von Nägeli (1817–1891). Nägeli was one of the most highly admired botanists of the mid-nineteenth century. Far from encouraging, however, Nägeli's letter of response expressed his skepticism of Mendel's ideas.

This may have been disappointing to Mendel, but he continued to write to Nägeli. Much of what we know today about Mendel comes from the letters that he wrote to Nägeli. The two men wrote to each other for seven years, but Nägeli never accepted Mendel's findings.

A SHORTENED SCIENTIFIC CAREER

Mendel never published another scientific paper after 1866. In 1868, Abbot Napp died and Mendel was selected to succeed him. As abbot, Mendel was very busy. Although his interest in biology continued, he did not have time for further research with his plants. Scientific work became a leisure activity for him.

As abbot, Mendel became a skilled administrator. He was patient, logical, thorough, and creative. The strengths that Mendel had once used to conduct research in heredity he now used to govern the men in his monastery. Although the monastery may have gained a hardworking and devoted abbot, the scientific world had lost a brilliant investigator.

As Mendel grew older, his health began to fail. He died of Bright disease, a chronic deterioration of the kidneys, on January 6, 1884, when he was just sixty-one. Although Mendel died well respected by all who knew him, he was little known in science. He would never know that he would come to be considered one of the greatest scientists of the nineteenth century.

The ultimate irony was that there was one man who would have recognized the importance of Mendel's work right away if he had read it. Charles Darwin knew that the biggest flaw in his theory of evolution was his inadequate theory of inheritance. When Darwin died in 1882, a copy of the issue of *Proceedings of the Natural History Society of Brünn* with Mendel's paper was found on his bookshelf. However, it had never been opened. He had never read it.

MENDEL REDISCOVERED

Mendel was understandably discouraged by the lack of attention that his paper received. He was the first person to understand the importance of applying mathematics to a biological problem. This was a strange idea to the

DUTCH BOTANIST HUGO DE VRIES, SHOWN HERE IN 1933, WAS ONE OF THREE PROMINENT SCIENTISTS WHOSE EXPERIMENTS IN THE LATE NINETEENTH CENTURY REVEALED THE LAWS OF HEREDITY. WHILE WORKING ON THE PUBLICATION OF THEIR RESULTS IN 1900, THOSE SCIENTISTS DISCOVERED THAT MENDEL HAD PUBLISHED SIMILAR CONCLUSIONS MORE THAN THIRTY YEARS EARLIER. THEY ALL GAVE MENDEL CREDIT, THOUGH DE VRIES DID SO RELUCTANTLY.

scientists of that time. Mendel may have wondered if his ideas would ever be appreciated.

In fact, it was not until sixteen years after Mendel's death that the significance of his work was finally recognized. At the end of the nineteenth century, three scientists from three different countries began trying to figure out the laws of heredity by doing experiments with plants. These scientists were Hugo de Vries (1848–1935) of Holland, Carl Erich Correns (1864–1933) of Germany, and Erich Tschermak von Seysenegg (1871–1962) of Austria. All three independently reached the same conclusion and published it at about the same time in 1900.

Each one recognized that he had made a scientific breakthrough. All three prepared to

AFTER MENDEL'S WORK WAS REDISCOVERED, HE BECAME KNOWN AS THE FATHER OF GENETICS. BUT DURING HIS LIFE, HE EARNED THE TITLE OF ABBOT OF THE MONASTERY OF ST. THOMAS IN BRÜNN, SYMBOLIZED BY THE BLOOMING FUCHSIA FLOWER IN HIS HAND IN THIS OFFICIAL PORTRAIT.

publish their findings. And all three found the same surprise as they reviewed the literature. In the obscure *Proceedings of the Natural History Society of Brünn* of 1866, they discovered a report about heredity that drew the same conclusions that they did. The scientists shared their work but gave credit to Mendel for getting there first. (De Vries gave Mendel credit only after Correns criticized him for not doing so.)

When Mendel finally received the recognition he deserved, it went far beyond anything he had anticipated during his lifetime. Mendel became known as the Father of Genetics, and his mathematical description of heredity achieved the lofty title of Mendel's laws of inheritance.

CHAPTER FIVE

MENDEL'S LAWS AND GENES

Mendel's laws, though mathematical, are much more than numbers and calculations. Mendel's laws are scientific principles that he deduced from careful analysis of his collection of data. Those principles describe how the characteristics of pea plants are passed down from parents to their offspring. Mendel concluded that parents pass traits to their offspring by basic units that he called heredity factors.

Mendel concluded that heredity factors remain unchanged during the lifetime of an organism and so could be passed on to generation after generation. Today we know those factors as genes, and we know that Mendel's laws apply to all forms of life on Earth—including humans.

GENE PAIRS

From his crossbreeding experiments, Mendel concluded that each plant had a pair of heredity factors for each trait, with one contributed by each parent. For instance, each plant had two factors for height, two factors for seed color, two factors for seed shape, and so forth. But when the plant produced its sex cells, each sex cell included only one factor for each of the traits.

Mendel brought together the sex cells from two different plants when he transferred the pollen. These pure-breeding plants had two factors for the same trait—two short or two tall factors, for example. Each

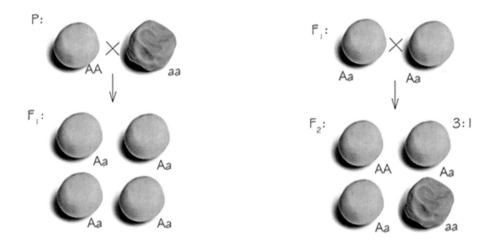

was sure to pass on a factor for its trait. Crossing the two plants resulted in offspring that each had one tall factor and one short factor.

Since crossing a tall pea plant with a short one produced offspring that were all tall, Mendel knew that heredity was not simply a matter of blending the factors from each parent. If the idea of blending were correct, Mendel would have gotten all medium-sized plants. To explain the 3:1 ratio that he had discovered,

THE 3:1 RATIO AND BEYOND

Mendel realized that the hybrids in the first generation would produce sex cells with the tall and short traits in equal numbers. So the next generation of pea plants, produced by mating the hybrids, had equal numbers of tall-tall, tall-short, short-tall, and short-short combinations. Since the tall trait was dominant, the first three combinations produced tall offspring, and the last produced short offspring. That led Mendel to expect the 3:1 ratio, and his expectation was shown to be correct in his experimental results.

Mendel could then go further in his experiments. If his conclusions about dominance were correct, the short peas in the second generation would have to be true breeders for the short trait. But only one-third of the tall plants (the ones that inherited the tall trait from both parents) were true breeders for the tall trait. The others inherited one of each trait and were hybrids for that trait, just as both their parent plants were.

he suggested that one of the heredity factors for a particular trait was "dominant," or stronger, than the other factor for that trait. He called the weaker trait "recessive."

Because all the hybrid offspring of crossed tall and short pea plants were tall, Mendel concluded that the tall factor was dominant and the short factor was recessive. When a plant possessed both a tall and a short factor, the tall factor overpowered the short factor. The short trait had not disappeared, however. It had simply not been visible. When the hybrids produced their own sex cells to pass to the next generation, half of those cells carried the short trait. If two hybrids were mated and both of the joined sex cells carried the short trait, the resulting plant would be short. This is one of the laws of genetics as we understand it today.

WHERE THE GENES ARE

Although Mendel was the first to describe heredity factors, which we now call genes, his research did not reveal how those factors were contained in the sex cells. To do that required research into cells that began by looking at them under a microscope.

When scientists did that with plant and animal cells, they discovered smaller structures inside each cell. Those are now called organelles. The largest organelle, and the first to be discovered, is called the nucleus. The nucleus is the control center of the cell. Inside the nucleus are

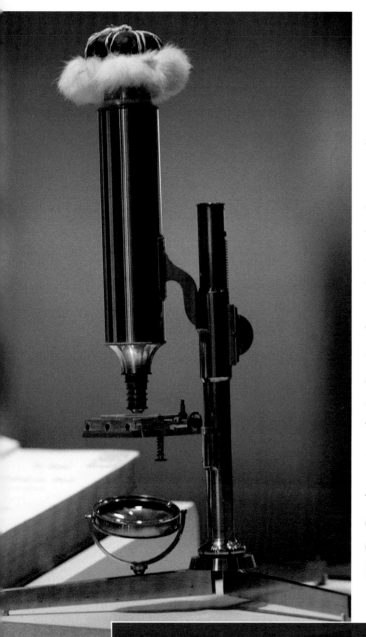

tiny structures called chromosomes. Scientists discovered chromosomes by studying the process of cell division, known as mitosis. As the nucleus splits in half, pairs of chromosomes become visible, double themselves, and separate to form nuclei of two new cells, each identical to the original one.

That is true of all the types of cells in the body except the sex cells. They are formed in a process called meiosis, in which the chromosome pairs separate instead of doubling. The sex cells contain only one of each pair, or half the number of chromosomes in the other body cells.

VILLANOVA UNIVERSITY PRESENTS AN ANNUAL MENDEL MEDAL THAT RECOGNIZES A SCIENTIST WHOSE WORK DEMONSTRATES THE COMPATIBILITY OF SCIENTIFIC ACHIEVEMENT AND RELIGIOUS CONVICTION. IN 2008, FOR THE EIGHTIETH ANNIVERSARY PRESENTATION OF THE MEDAL, THE UNIVERSITY DECLARED THE UPCOMING ACADEMIC YEAR AS THE YEAR OF MENDEL AND SPONSORED A TRAVELING EXHIBIT THAT FEATURED MENDEL'S MICROSCOPE.

When you compare those processes to Mendel's laws of inheritance, you realize that chromosomes must carry the inherited traits. The pairs are one chromosome from the organism's male parent and one matching chromosome from its female parent. When the organism uses meiosis to produce its own sex cells to pass along a trait, such as tall or small, it doesn't pass along a mixture of its parents' traits, but rather the trait of only one of its parents.

With more research, scientists were able to identify that certain traits were carried on certain chromosomes. In fact, a chromosome could be responsible for more than one trait. That means that each chromosome carries several of Mendel's heredity factors, which we now call genes. (We will use the modern terminology—genes instead of heredity factors—from here on.)

Every organism has an even number of chromosomes in each of its body cells, half from its female parent and half from its male parent. Different species have different numbers. Humans have forty-six chromosomes, gorillas forty-eight, and pea plants fourteen. The sex cells have half the number of chromosomes of body cells, so a human sex cell has twenty-three chromosomes.

The plants that Mendel worked with had sex cells, just like humans do. When Mendel transferred pollen from one plant to another, he was bringing together the sex cells of the two plants. Each plant's sex cell had seven chromosomes, so the resulting pea plants all had seven pairs of chromosomes, for a total of fourteen chromosomes in each cell.

Each chromosome can have thousands of genes on it, and the genes guide the way an organism develops. Because of your genes, you have a human body structure and human organs. Your genes told your body how to grow. What color are your eyes? Is your hair straight or curly? Do you have freckles? Do you have big feet? These things all developed under the control of your genes.

WHY YOU RESEMBLE YOUR PARENTS AND GRANDPARENTS

You received your genes from your parents. You may look a little bit like each of your parents. That is because one sex cell from your father joined with a sex cell from your mother to make you. When your parents' sex cells joined together, you received twenty-three chromosomes from each of them. Each cell in your

THIS SMILING TEENAGER AND HER GRANDMOTHER LOOK ALIKE IN MANY WAYS AND PROBABLY SHARE SOME PERSONALITY TRAITS THAT ARE CARRIED IN HUMAN GENES. ONE TRAIT THAT THE GRANDMOTHER PROBABLY PASSED DOWN TO THE GRANDDAUGHTER IS EYE COLOR. THE ALLELE FOR BLUE EYES IS RECESSIVE, SO THE GRANDDAUGHTER HAD TO INHERIT IT FROM BOTH OF HER PARENTS.

body now has twenty-three pairs of chromosomes, for a total of forty-six chromosomes in each cell. One chromosome of each pair came from your mother, while the other chromosome came from your father.

Each of your parents got half of their chromosomes from each of their parents. That means that your forty-six chromosomes can be traced back to four grandparents. That's why you look like them in certain ways and often share similar personality traits or ways of thinking.

GENES AND ALLELES

Mendel's experiments turned out to be simple in a particular way. Each of the seven pea traits he studied was connected with a single gene. One gene was responsible for seed color, another for plant height, another for seed shape, and so forth. Each trait was expressed in the plant in one of two different ways. The plants could be tall or short. The seeds could be smooth or wrinkled. The seeds could be green or yellow.

Mendel's most important discovery was that a plant's traits were controlled not by single genes but by pairs, one from each parent. The same gene could come in one of several different variations. Each variation is what we now call an allele.

For example, Mendel discovered that the gene for plant height had two possible alleles—tall or short—though he did not use that term. Any one plant had

SEX CELLS AND COIN FLIPS

People get twenty-three of their forty-six chromosomes from each parent. It's an even split between the mother and father. But nature isn't as fair to grandparents. To produce a sex cell, the process of meiosis selects one chromosome at random from each pair in that person's genetic makeup. Each particular chromosome in that sex cell has a 50-50 chance of coming from the person's mother and a 50-50 chance of coming from the person's father. It's like flipping a coin. After twenty-three flips the result is usually eleven or twelve of each heads and tails—a balance between the grandparents on that side of the family. But it could split 15–8—or even 23–0, which only happens once in more than four million times.

two height genes, one from each parent. If either gene had the tall allele, the plant grew tall. Some tall plants carried a short allele, but they didn't express it in their body. However, each sex cell those plants produced had a 50-50 chance of passing along the short allele.

He also saw that the gene for flower color had at least two alleles—one allele for white and one allele for purple. When Mendel crossed two pure-breeding plants, a copy of only one allele was passed from each parent. The offspring ended up with one allele for each trait. Its flowers were purple, but it had a 50-50 chance of passing on the allele for white flowers to its descendants.

FROM PEAS TO PEOPLE

Just like pea plants, humans receive two copies of each of their genes, one from each parent. For a gene that comes in more than one allele, the gene pair may have two different alleles. In some cases, the traits produced by those alleles are different in obvious ways. Those include eye color and hair color and type.

For example, the allele for brown eyes is dominant, while the allele for blue eyes is recessive. If a child receives an allele for blue eyes from one parent but an allele for brown eyes from the other parent, that child will have brown eyes. The child could have blue eyes only if he or she received blue-eyed alleles from both parents. This can happen even if both parents are brown-eyed themselves, if they have recessive blue-eyed alleles in their genes.

Inheritance in most organisms, however, is much more complex than in Mendel's peas. In many cases, the traits are less clear. For example, several genes influence a person's growth rate and adult height, and several others influence different mental abilities, such as skills in language or mathematics. Also, it is not necessary for one allele to be dominant. Sometimes, the two alleles can compromise to produce something in between. For example, when red snapdragons are crossed with white snapdragons, the first generation of hybrids is pink.

PARENTS PASS MANY TRAITS AND TALENTS TO THEIR CHILDREN THROUGH THEIR GENES. BUT BEYOND OBVIOUS TRAITS LIKE SKIN OR EYE COLOR, MUCH OF A CHILD'S DEVELOPMENT DEPENDS ON ENVIRONMENTAL AND SOCIAL INFLUENCES, A FACT THAT THIS FATHER CLEARLY UNDERSTANDS.

These results do not prove the blending theory, however. The blending theory says that once the red and white traits are combined, they would not be seen separately in later generations. In the case of the snapdragons, the plants with pink flowers carry one red and one white allele. When they are crossed, only half the offspring get one red and one white allele.

Those produce pink flowers like their parents. One fourth of the offspring get two red alleles and produce red flowers. And the remaining one fourth get two white alleles and produce white flowers.

We also now know that there are instances when two alleles are both fully expressed or there are more than two alleles for a certain gene. This occurs with human blood type, for example. There are alleles for type A, type B, or neither. A person gets one allele from each parent and the result is that human blood types can be A, B, AB (both A and B alleles), or O (neither A nor B alleles).

Another human trait, skin color, is determined by how much of the pigment melanin the body produces. Each person has two gene pairs (four alleles) that control the production of melanin. This results in skin colors ranging from very light to medium to very dark.

YOU-NIQUE

Scientists have now determined that humans have between twenty thousand and twenty-five thousand different genes. Most of these genes have at least two alleles. Even though family members may resemble each other, none of them looks exactly alike because there are so many different ways that alleles can be combined.

Even though there are more than seven billion people on Earth, no two people look exactly alike or have exactly the same genes, except for identical twins. Identical twins result when a fertilized egg divides into two instead of creating one embryo with two cells. (An embryo is the first stage of an organism's development.) Each embryo goes on to develop into a baby. Since both babies come from the same egg, they have the same exact genes.

Because of slight differences in their development in the mother's womb, even identical twins do not look exactly alike. But those differences are very hard to notice. They are indeed the "spitting image" of each other at birth. Even as they become slightly different as they grow, their genes will always be the same. But unless you have an identical sibling, you are the only person in the world with your particular set of genes and alleles. There never was a person with genes exactly like yours, and there never will be one in the future. You are unique not just for now but in all human history, including the times to come.

CHAPTER SIX

GENETICS SINCE MENDEL

Mendel's work on the science of inheritance ended in the mid-nineteenth century and was not rediscovered until the twentieth century began. Soon after that, the word "gene" entered the vocabulary of science, replacing Mendel's terminology of "heredity factor." Sources vary about the date, but they agree that Danish chemist Wilhelm Ludvig Johannsen (1857–1927) coined the word "gene," as well as several related words.

According to a historical note that appeared in 2002 in the scientific journal *Hormones*, Johannsen first used the word in 1902 and based it on *genos*, meaning "seed" in Greek. He drew it from the writings of the Greek physician Hippocrates (460 BCE–375 BCE), who is considered the father of rational medicine. In the following century, the science of genetics came of age, and it has become even more important in the twenty-first century.

THE BIOLOGY AND CHEMISTRY OF INHERITANCE

Mendel's work had established that biological inheritance in plants was carried by genes and transmitted by the joining of two sex cells, one each from the male and female portions of the plant. And it was clear that the same process of heredity took place in animals. But what was in the sex cells that caused that process to take place?

By 1915, Thomas Hunt Morgan (1866–1945) had discovered that genes were arranged on chromosomes. In 1944, Oswald Avery

THOMAS HUNT MORGAN, SHOWN HERE, RECEIVED THE 1933 NOBEL PRIZE IN PHYSIOLOGY OR MEDICINE FOR HIS 1915 DISCOVERY THAT AN ORGANISM'S GENES ARE ARRANGED ON ITS CHROMOSOMES. IN 1944, OSWALD AVERY, MACLYN MCCARTY, AND COLIN M. MACLEOD DISCOVERED THAT THE CHROMOSOMES ARE PART OF A LARGE MOLECULE CALLED DEOXYRIBONUCLEIC ACID, OR DNA.

(1877–1955), Maclyn McCarty, (1911–2005) and Colin M. MacLeod (1909–1972) determined that inheritance in pneumonia bacteria is carried on large molecules called deoxyribonucleic acid (DNA).

Bacteria are an important class of single-celled life forms that don't have nuclei or other organelles. But scientists already knew that DNA is the substance in

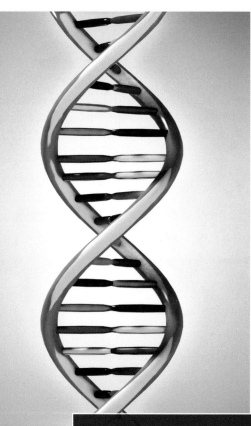

the nuclei of plant and animal cells. So it was clear that those large molecules somehow carried chromosomes and genes for all forms of life. But what was it about DNA that enabled it to hold genes, and how did those genes function in the bodies of living organisms?

The answers finally began to emerge from the research of James Watson (1928–), Francis Crick (1916–2004), and other scientists, most notably Maurice Wilkins (1916–2004) and Rosalind Franklin (1920–1958). In 1953, they discovered that a

AFTER THE DISCOVERY THAT DNA HELD THE RECIPE FOR LIFE, SCIENTISTS WONDERED HOW IT WORKED. FURTHER RESEARCH SHOWED THAT IT WAS MADE UP OF SMALLER MOLECULES—SUGARS, PHOSPHATES, AND FOUR CHEMICAL BASES. IN 1953, ROSALIND FRANKLIN AND MAURICE WILKINS AT KINGS COLLEGE IN LONDON USED THE TECHNIQUE OF X-RAY CRYSTALLOGRAPHY TO REVEAL THE SPIRAL-STAIRCASE STRUCTURE OF DNA, AND JAMES WATSON AND FRANCIS CRICK OF CAMBRIDGE UNIVERSITY FIGURED OUT HOW THE VARIOUS SMALLER MOLECULES WERE ARRANGED TO CREATE A CODE FOR BUILDING THE ENTIRE ORGANISM.

DNA molecule had a structure like a spiral ladder or staircase. The mathematical name for that shape is a double helix. A helix is the shape of a coil spring.

In the DNA molecule, the two helixes that form the backbone of the ladder are made of alternating sugars and phosphates. Joining them are chemical rungs that can be one of four different types of nucleotides or bases. If you follow the rungs up the ladder, you are reading a message written in a four-letter chemical language. The message is an instruction book for the body, and the instructions are the genes!

USING GENETICS TO TREAT DISEASE

Once scientists understood Mendel's laws and the role of DNA in genetics, they began using their knowledge to understand inherited diseases. In many cases, a child develops a disease only when both parents carry a recessive allele for the condition and pass it along to the child. It's the same situation that leads to blue eyes, except that the consequences are harmful.

An example is the sickle cell trait that is common in people of African descent. This trait changes the shape of red blood cells and affects the blood's ability to carry oxygen. It turns out that having one sickle cell allele and one normal allele protects a person from getting malaria without affecting the red blood cells.

PEOPLE WHO INHERIT THE SICKLE CELL ALLELE FROM ONLY ONE PARENT ARE RESISTANT TO A TROPICAL DISEASE CALLED MALARIA. BUT IN PEOPLE WHO INHERIT THAT ALLELE FROM BOTH PARENTS, THE RED BLOOD CELLS SOMETIMES TAKE A SHAPE RESEMBLING THE CURVED BLADE OF A SICKLE. BECAUSE SICKLE CELLS DO NOT CARRY OXYGEN WELL, THOSE PEOPLE CAN DEVELOP A CONDITION THAT RESEMBLES ANEMIA, IN WHICH A PERSON'S BLOOD HAS TOO FEW RED CELLS.

Inheriting one sickle cell allele provided an advantage to people living where malaria was common, as it is in much of Africa. But if a person inherits the allele from both parents, that person will develop the sickle cell trait. By taking precautions, a person with the sickle cell trait can have a long life. But many other genetic conditions caused by inheriting two "bad" alleles lead to greatly shortened or seriously impaired lives.

Some genetic diseases occur even if the person inherits only one allele for the condition. One of the worst of these is Huntington's disease. People with Huntington's usually begin losing control of their muscles at around the age of forty. That is followed by dementia that worsens as time passes. Huntington's victims rarely live much past fifty. But by the time they show symptoms of the disease, they may have had children. Each child has a 50 percent chance of developing the disease, too.

Thanks to genetics research, scientists have now identified the genes that cause many serious genetic illnesses, including Huntington's disease. That is often the first step in developing treatments to slow the progression of a disease or control the symptoms. In the case of certain particularly devastating diseases, some adults in high-risk groups choose to have their genetic makeup tested before having children.

If both potential parents carry a harmful recessive trait, they may choose to have children by in vitro fertilization. In that process, a woman's sex cell (an egg or ovum) is fertilized by the man's sex cell (sperm) outside of her body. A laboratory tests the genes of the resulting embryo to make sure it has not inherited both harmful alleles. If doctors find the embryo will not have the disease, they transfer it to the woman's body, and she becomes pregnant with a child who will not have the harmful trait.

MAPPING THE HUMAN GENOME

DNA scientists have gone far beyond just finding which genes reside on which chromosomes. They have developed techniques that can read the sequence of the rungs on a DNA molecule, and they know what types of sequences can make a gene.

The whole set of genes of an organism is called its genome. In 1990, the National Institutes of Health (NIH) opened a research center, now known as the National Human Genome Research Institute (NHGRI), to conduct the Human Genome Project. The object was to produce a complete sequence of

DR. PETER LICHTER OF YALE MEDICAL SCHOOL MAPS PART OF A HUMAN GENOME, USING A TECHNIQUE KNOWN AS NONRADIOACTIVE IN-SITU HYBRIDIZATION. THE RED OBJECTS ON HIS SCREEN ARE CHROMOSOMES. THE GREEN-YELLOW COLOR SHOWS WHERE A CERTAIN DNA SEQUENCE, WHICH MAY BE A PARTICULAR GENE OR A KNOWN MARKER FOR A TRAIT, APPEARS ON THE CHROMOSOME.

human DNA within fifteen years. Scientists met that goal in 2003 with two years to spare and produced an official estimate of the number of genes to be between twenty thousand and twenty-five thousand. That number was about half of the original estimate.

By 2012 some companies were offering genome mapping for a partial set of genes in individuals at a cost of under $100. While in 2013 the cost of mapping a complete human genome was still thousands of dollars, numerous companies were racing to develop a lower-cost method.

GENETIC ENGINEERING AND GENE THERAPY

When Mendel did his experiments with peas, he didn't change the genes of the sex cells he united to produce new plants. But modern science and technology have made it possible to take a gene from one organism and put it into the DNA of another. That is called genetic engineering. It is being used quite successfully in agriculture, and many people are very pleased with its results and possibilities. But for some others, the techniques of genetic engineering are very controversial. They refuse to eat genetically modified food and don't think it should be produced or sold at all. That is often the case in technology, and it often takes a long time for societies to decide what is most sensible for them.

Scientists are also considering a controversial approach to treating genetic diseases by treating a person's body cells directly. Called gene therapy, its goal is to replace or deactivate a gene that causes serious illness, or to add a new gene to the cells. At present, gene therapy is considered highly experimental.

Mendel never could have anticipated that the research in his small monastery garden would lead to both wonderful developments in medicine and controversial developments in technology. But then he never could have imagined that his results would be considered revolutionary. Looking at what we still have to learn about genes and genetics at present, many people would say that the revolution is only beginning.

TIMELINE

1822 Gregor Mendel is born in Heinzendorf, Moravia.

1833 Mendel goes to school in Leipnik.

1834 Mendel enters the gymnasium in Troppau.

1840 Mendel graduates from the gymnasium in Troppau. He begins his studies at the Philosophical Institute at Olmütz.

1843 Mendel joins the Augustinian monastery of St. Thomas in Brünn. He takes on the name Gregor.

1847 Mendel is ordained into the priesthood.

1849 Mendel begins teaching at the secondary school at Znaim.

1850 Mendel enters the University of Vienna.

1854 Mendel begins his heredity experiments with pea plants in the garden of the Augustinian monastery.

1863 Mendel completes his experiments with peas.

1865 Mendel presents his findings to the Natural Science Society in Brünn.

1866 Mendel's paper, "Versuche über Pflanzen-Hybriden" ("Experiments on Plant Hybrids") appears in the journal *Proceedings of the Natural History Society of Brünn.*

1868 Abbot Napp dies and Mendel is elected to be the new abbot of the monastery in Brünn.

1884 Mendel dies.

1900 Hugo de Vries, Carl Erich Correns, and Erich Tschermak von Seysenegg rediscover Mendel and his work.

c. 1902 Wilhelm Ludvig Johannsen coins the word "gene."

1915 Thomas Hunt Morgan discovers that genes lie on chromosomes.

1944 Oswald Avery, Maclyn McCarty, and Colin M. MacLeod determine that inheritance in pneumonia bacteria is carried on large molecules called deoxyribonucleic acid (DNA).

1953 James Watson, Francis Crick, Maurice Wilkins, and Rosalind Franklin determine the structure of the DNA molecule.

1990 The Human Genome Project begins at the National Institutes of Health.

2003 The complete human genome is published.

2012–2013 Dozens of companies race to reduce the cost of sequencing an entire human genome to less than $1000.

ALLELE One of two or more different versions of the same gene.

CELL The basic unit that makes up living things.

CHROMOSOME One of several small structures that form on an organism's DNA when a cell begins to divide. Each chromosome carries many genes.

DEOXYRIBONUCLEIC ACID (DNA) A large molecule that is shaped like a spiral staircase or ladder and that is the basis for all life on Earth. The rungs of the ladder are a code built from four different chemical units called nucleotides or bases, which spell out the instructions for an organism's development and function.

DOMINANT GENE A gene that is expressed over a recessive gene in the same pair.

EMBRYO The earliest stage of development of a many-celled plant or animal.

EVOLUTION The theory that current species of organisms adapted to their environments through a process of gradual change.

FERTILIZATION The joining together of sex cells to form a new living thing.

GENE A unit of DNA that determines one aspect of heredity.

GENE THERAPY The treatment of certain disorders by replacing or deactivating faulty genes or by introducing other genes into the patient's cells.

GENETIC ENGINEERING The modification of organisms by artificially inserting new genes or replacing existing ones in seeds or embryos.

GENETICS The study of genes and heredity.

GENOME The full set of genes of an organism as encoded in that organism's DNA.

HEREDITY The passing of traits from parents to their offspring.

HYBRID The offspring of genetically dissimilar parents.

MEIOSIS The process of cell division that creates a sex cell. Meiosis passes on only one member of each chromosome pair in the original cell.

MITOSIS The division of a cell into two cells, each identical to the original.

NUCLEOTIDE A chemical unit that pairs with another unit to form a rung of the DNA ladder.

NUCLEUS The control center of a plant or animal cell, which contains genes, chromosomes, and DNA.

ORGANELLE A structure inside of a cell.

PEDAGOGY The study of teaching techniques.

RECESSIVE GENE The gene that is weaker than the dominant gene and that is not expressed when paired with a dominant gene.

STATISTICS The field of mathematics that deals with the description and analysis of sets of numerical data.

FOR MORE INFORMATION

Mendel Museum of Masaryk University

Augustinian Abbey in Old Brno

Mendlovo náměstí 1a

603 00 Brno

Czech Republic

Web site: http://www.mendelmuseum.muni.cz/en

This museum is devoted to the life and work of Mendel. It includes his scientific work and his work as a monk and abbot.

Museum of Science and Industry, Chicago

57th Street and Lake Shore Drive

Chicago, IL 60637-2093

(773) 684-1414

Web site: http://www.msichicago.org

One of the leading science museums in the United States, the Museum of Science and Industry has a large set of biology exhibits, including some on genetics and DNA.

National Museum of Natural History (NMNH)

P.O. Box 37012, Smithsonian Institution

Washington, DC 20013-7012

(202) 633-1000

Web site: http://www.mnh.si.edu

Part of the Smithsonian Institution, this museum has a variety of temporary and permanent exhibits on the life sciences. Its exhibition Genome: Unlocking Life's Code, created in collaboration with the National Human Genome Research Institute, presents key insights about the human genome.

Ontario Science Centre

770 Don Mills Road

Toronto, ON M3C 1T3

Canada

(416) 696-1000

Web site: http://www.ontariosciencecentre.ca

The Ontario Science Centre is one of North America's most popular and innovative science museums, with numerous exhibits and programs on the life sciences and technology.

The Tech Museum of Innovation

201 South Market Street

San Jose, CA 95113

(408) 294-8324

Web site: http://www.thetech.org

This museum focuses on technology and innovation, including the latest developments in genetics. Its mission is "to inspire the innovator in everyone." The museum's Web site offers a variety of educational resources on genetics at http://genetics.thetech.org.

WEB SITES

Due to the changing nature of Internet links, Rosen Publishing has developed an online list of Web sites related to the subject of this book. This site is updated regularly. Please use this link to access the list:

http://www.rosenlinks.com/SPRD/gmend

FOR FURTHER READING

Anderson, Michael. *A Closer Look at Genes and Genetic Engineering* (Introduction to Biology). New York, NY: Britannica Educational Publishing in association with Rosen Educational Services, 2012.

Cregan, Elizabeth R. *Pioneers in Cell Biology* (Mission: Science). Mankato, MN: Compass Point Books, 2010.

Day, Trevor. *Genetics: Investigating the Function of Genes and the Science of Heredity* (Scientific Pathways). New York, NY: Rosen Central, 2013.

Duke, Shirley Smith. *You Can't Wear These Genes* (Let's Explore Science). Vero Beach, FL: Rourke Publishing, 2011.

Eason, Sarah. *Reproduction and Genetics* (Facts at Your Fingertips). Tucson, AZ: Brown Bear Books, 2010.

Einspruch, Andrew. *DNA Detectives* (Discovery Education). New York, NY: PowerKids Press, 2013.

Farndon, John, Alex Woolf, Anne Rooney, and Liz Gogerly. *Great Scientists* (Great People in History). New York, NY: Rosen Publishing, 2013.

Gardner, Robert. *Genetics and Evolution Science Fair Projects: Revised and Expanded Using the Scientific Method.* Berkeley Heights, NJ: Enslow Publishers, 2010.

Green, Jen. *Inheritance and Reproduction* (Essential Life Science). Chicago, IL: Capstone Heinemann Library, 2014.

Guttman, Burton S. *Genetics: The Code of Life* (Contemporary Issues). New York, NY: Rosen Publishing, 2011.

Hand, Carol. *Introduction to Genetics* (Understanding Genetics). New York, NY: Rosen Publishing, 2011.

Heos, Bridget. *The Human Genome* (Understanding Genetics). New York, NY: Rosen Publishing, 2011.

O'Neal, Claire. *Projects in Genetics* (Life Science Projects for Kids). Hockessin, DE: Mitchell Lane Publishers, 2011.

Pringle, Laurence, Steve Jenkins, Jerry A. Coyne, and Carla Weise. *Billions of Years, Amazing Changes: The Story of Evolution*. Honesdale, PA: Boyds Mills, 2011.

Sandvold, Lynette Brent. *Genetics* (Big Ideas in Science). New York, NY: Marshall Cavendish Benchmark, 2010.

Schultz, Mark, Zander Cannon, and Kevin Cannon. *The Stuff of Life: A Graphic Guide to Genetics and DNA*. New York, NY: Hill and Wang, 2009.

Simpson, Kathleen, and Sarah Tishkoff. *Genetics: From DNA to Designer Dogs* (National Geographic Investigates). Washington, DC: National Geographic, 2008.

Van Gorp, Lynn. *Gregor Mendel: Genetics Pioneer* (Mission: Science). Mankato, MN: Compass Point Books, 2009.

BIBLIOGRAPHY

Aaseng, Nathan. *Genetics: Unlocking the Secrets of Life* (Innovators). Minneapolis, MN: Oliver Press, 1996.

Augnet.org. "Gregor Mendel." 2010. Retrieved April 9, 2013 (http://www.augnet.org/?ipageid=777).

Corcos, Alain F., and Floyd V. Monaghan. *Gregor Mendel's Experiments on Plant Hybrids: A Guided Study.* New Brunswick, NJ: Rutgers University Press, 1993.

Edelson, Edward. *Gregor Mendel and the Roots of Genetics.* New York, NY: Oxford University Press, 1999.

Henig, Robin Marantz. *The Monk in the Garden: The Lost and Found Genius of Gregor Mendel, the Father of Genetics.* Boston, MA: Houghton Mifflin Company, 2000.

Kean, Sam. *The Violinist's Thumb: And Other Lost Tales of Love, War, and Genius, as Written by Our Genetic Code.* New York, NY: Little, Brown and Co., 2012.

Kontopoulou, Theano D., and Spyros G. Marketos. "Tracing the Origin of the Term 'Gene.'" *Hormones*, 2003. Retrieved April 9, 2013 (http://www.hormones.gr/140/article/article.html).

McCarty, Maclyn. "Discovering Genes Are Made of DNA." *Nature* 421, January 2003, p. 406.

Nivet, C. "1848: Gregor Mendel, the Monk Who Wanted to Be a Citizen." *Med Sci*, April 2006, pp. 430–433.

PBS.org. "The Thousand-Dollar Genome." January 25, 2013. Retrieved April 9, 2013 (http://www

.pbs.org/wnet/religionandethics/episodes/january
-25-2013/the-thousand-dollar-genome/14569/).

Ridley, Matt. *Genome: The Autobiography of a Species in 23 Chapters.* New York, NY: HarperCollins, 2000.

Snedden, Robert. *The History of Genetics.* New York, NY: Thomson Learning, 1995.

Sootin, Harry. *Gregor Mendel: Father of the Science of Genetics.* New York, NY: Vanguard Press, 1959.

Tudge, Colin. *The Impact of the Gene: From Mendel's Peas to Designer Babies.* New York, NY: Hill and Wang, 2001.

U.S. Department of Energy Genome Programs. "Human Genome Project Information." Retrieved April 9, 2013 (http://www.ornl.gov/sci/techresources/ Human_Genome/home.shtml).

U.S. National Library of Medicine. "What Is Gene Therapy?" Genetics Home Reference, April 1, 2013. Retrieved April 9, 2013 (http://ghr.nlm .nih.gov/handbook/therapy/genetherapy).

INDEX

ABOUT THE AUTHOR

After earning his Ph.D. at Carnegie Mellon University in 1971, physicist Fred Bortz set off on an interesting and varied twenty-five-year career in teaching and research. From 1979 to 1994, he was on staff at Carnegie Mellon, where his work evolved from research to outreach.

After his third book, *Catastrophe! Great Engineering Failure—and Success*, was designated a "Selector's Choice" on the 1996 list of Outstanding Science Trade Books for Children, he decided to spend the rest of his career as a full-time writer. His books, now numbering nearly thirty, have since won awards, including the American Institute of Physics Science Writing Award, and recognition on several best books lists.

Known on the Internet as the smiling, bowtie-wearing "Dr. Fred," he welcomes inquisitive visitors to his Web site at http://www.fredbortz.com.

PHOTO CREDITS